Table of Contents

7 Ways Effective Speakers Communicate Their Message and Keep the Audience Happy, Engaged, and Interested...

Leigh Miller was excited when she was asked to speak to a work group about an area of her expertise.

She had prepared her data and facts and had given what she considered a wealth of information to a receptive crowd.

But she was left with the unsettling feeling that she had somehow lost them.

She felt confused and poured over her presentation trying to figure out how or where she could have gotten derailed.

In the end she couldn't put her finger on one specific moment that had lost her the audience. Instead, it felt like a culmination of things throughout her talk that her audience was unable to identify with.

Communication Tip #1 – Define your niche topic so you come across focused and professional

Look at choosing your niche the same way you would if you had created a product. Say you are creating a gadget that solves a specific problem.

You know your gadget can't be all things to all people. However, you also know that one, specific person will welcome the benefits your gadget presents.

So you formulate your marketing plan geared to that one, specific buyer.

You can apply the same thinking to defining your speaking niche. Your message will solve a specific problem for a specific type of person, or it will motivate and instruct them how to solve it themselves.

Both your message and your audience are two equal parts of the same equation. Your perspective or your niche is what makes the message come alive and you have to be absolutely clear about what it is.

If your audience wants general information, they can go to the internet or read a book. But if they've come out to see you speak, they want to hear specific, benefit-driven information on your area of expertise.

If you don't know what your niche is, then it's time to start asking questions.

If your topic is **work related** or *informative* – ask a trusted colleague or friend what you do better than anyone else. What specific information do you have that people would pay a fair price for to have or know? Do you know a short cut to getting something done extremely well, and in less time than others? Chances are people would appreciate hearing about it.

Even if you are sharing factual or academic information, you can still put your spin on it to make it your own. Ask 10 people to draw the same happy face picture; you'll get 10 different pictures. Our perspectives are what make us unique and interesting.

Think about your hobbies. What do you love to do and in what area have you become really skilled? Hobbyists are always looking for the latest tricks and tips for doing something they already love.

Do you volunteer your time? Are you active in humanitarian endeavours? Is there something that really lights you up that people should know about and participate in? Share it!

Do you have a particularly entertaining or engaging event or experience people would find interesting to learn more about? But make sure it's exciting! No one wants to hear about your trip to the grocery store.

Once you tap into your niche topic from your own perspective, you will be identified as the expert in that area that people love to listen to.

I used to listen to a radio program that had a financial report read by a woman who clearly had no radio training.

Besides financial statistics being a bit of a dry topic to begin with, the woman's lack of personality on the air made her reports flat-out boring, like listening to an automated voice message recap of a grocery list.

Over time, she obviously got some coaching because she started putting her personality (which changed her vocal inflection) into her readings. Before long, I actually looked forward to listening to her. It became interesting because she had put her individuality into it.

This is the level of engagement that you should be shooting for!

Communication Tip #2 – Identify what speaker type you are to avoid audience confusion and uncertainty

A speaker trying to be everything to all people is like preparing a meal with every spice thrown in… savory, sweet, exotic. It won't have any one specific flavor, and in the end it will only leave a bad taste in your mouth.

Bottom line – you can't change your speaker type based on who you're speaking to, and you shouldn't even try. The answer? … Simply choose which one you would like to be.

The Four Types of Speakers:

If you've been asked to speak at an event where the audience primarily just listens and doesn't take notes – you're a *keynote*.

If you put the audience to work, and they're taking notes and you are giving them activities – you're a *facilitator*.

If you've been asked to provide a formal report on your expertise in a specific research area – you are an *academic/informational speaker*.

If you're a person people come to see because you're famous, and they just want to hear about you or your experiences – you're a **celebrity** and your journey to fame is what they came for.

That's not to say you can't have multiple speech types. For example, you can still be a keynote AND a facilitator, or an academic speaker AND a keynote, or whatever types you like. The point is for each speaker event and speech you have to choose one type only.

I once hired a keynote speaker who became famous from her horrific experience of having been kidnapped and tortured for 16 months. She introduced her topic by letting the audience know she would not be sharing or discussing details of her imprisonment or mistreatment because she didn't want the result of her talk to leave the audience feeling hatred for the men she chose to forgive. The audience accepted her request and didn't ask questions about her imprisonment. Hers was a beautiful example of handling a sensitive topic and the audience with dignity and respect.

Communication Tip #3 – Identify your speech type to create a lasting impression on your audience

Begin your talk with the end in mind. Once your audience has finished listening to you–what do you want them to do? Ponder the information? Take some sort of specific action? Or do you want to make them laugh and go home with a good feeling? Either way, the end goal is your choice and you need to know what it is before you begin.

Figuring this out is just as important as identifying your niche, because knowing what outcome you want from your audience will help you determine your speech type.

Plus, knowing your speech type goes a long way to figuring out how you will work with your audience…

If the main purpose of your talk is to give your audience information – your speech type is *informative*.

TIPS FOR KEYNOTES
Since many keynotes happen after lunch or dinner, keep your presentation material tight, fast-paced and entertaining. Figure 45 minutes as a good time frame – and 30 minutes will work even better. It's better to leave them wanting for more than putting them to sleep after a full meal.

TIPS FOR ACADEMICS
Know your facts and figures cold, and be prepared to be challenged by the audience. Practice taking in their comments and working with them, or throwing them back to the audience for discussion as opposed to arguing with them. Remember your audience is your client— treat them and their opinions with respect.

TIPS FOR FACILITATORS
Have interactive, interesting and fun activities throughout your presentation that take your audience on a journey of discovery of your main points or arguments.

TIPS FOR CELEBRITY SPEAKERS
Share the story of your personal journey that led to your success. If you've been involved in a scandal, think through how you will handle it or frame it within your speech so that the audience knows how you will deal with it and their questions concerning it.

HERE ARE SOME INTRODUCTION TECHNIQUES:

Tell a story – Everyone loves a good story and it's one of the most effective ways to engage your audience. Of course, make sure the story supports the topic or opinion you're presenting.

Ask a question – Whether the question is rhetorical or not, asking a question immediately challenges your audience to come up with an answer and keeps them focused on the subject matter.

Use a quote – Use quotes from other experts as proof of your claims or to validate your opinions.

Tell a joke/use humor – Like a good story, everyone enjoys a humorous moment. Jokes and humorous stories immediately engage an audience's interest – just keep it clean and make sure there's a good punchline!

If you want to win your audience over to an opinion or cause – your speech type is **persuasive**.

If your topic's goal is to entertain – your speech type is **entertaining**.

If your speech type announces news or information – your speech type is **news/announcement**.

Communication Tip #4 – Divide your talk into clearly defined sections that present a logical flow of information and keep your audience from getting confused

Have you ever attended a lecture, speaker event, or meeting where you sat and listened for an hour and at the end found yourself wondering what the point was?

I'll bet you didn't appreciate having the speaker waste your time.

Unfortunately this happens all too often, with the audience left wondering why they came in the first place.

It's not the audience's job to figure out the logic and flow of a talk – that's your job. It's also your job to organize it well enough so they don't get lost or frustrated trying to figure out where you're going.

So how do you organize your speech? Think back to high school English class where they showed you the structure of an essay. Writing a speech essentially follows the same format.

Every clear message has an introduction, a body, and a conclusion.

Yes, there are 2-3 sub points within each section as well as transitions, but if you leave the introduction, body, or conclusion out of your speech, both you and your audience will find yourselves out at sea fishing for your message.

It's really quite simple when you break it down to three sections:

1. The **introduction** has three basic goals:

   • To grab the audience's attention and warm them to your topic

   • To show your audience what's in it for them

   • To set yourself up as an expert and build a connection with your audience

2. The body is the middle and main section of your talk where you cover all the points from your experience and research to support the views of your topic. It should include these features:

   - One idea or main point per section/discussion
   - 1-3 sub points that qualify the main point
   - A logical sequence or progression of your ideas
   - Support/proof of your statements
   - Links or transitions between sections

3. The conclusion's main purpose is to summarize your point/theme, and convince the audience of your argument/perspective. It usually has the following information:

   - A summary of the main points/topic without bringing in any new material
   - A call to action

So there you have it. It's information you knew already, and all that's left for you to do is apply it to your own topic from your perspective.

Communication Tip #5 – Connect with your audience at their level to keep them interested and feeling like a part of the process

When you attended first grade your teacher took you on a journey from step one to a place where you were able to move on to the next level with confidence (that is, if you had a good teacher!).

She/he didn't assume you had completed any schooling beyond what she/he was teaching you. Chances are while you were being taught, you learned and understood the lessons being presented without your teacher talking down to you.

Those first experiences make all the difference in how we feel today about a subject or the teacher.

Although your audience may not be at a grade one level, they likely haven't spent their lifetime devoted to studying, researching, and working in your area.

Although your topic may or may not be new to them, you should attempt to take them on a fun and interesting discovery that leaves their hearts and minds open to understanding and embracing your subject matter.

By doing this you are showing them you care about the topic and about them, and in turn, they will warm to you and your topic.

HOW DO YOU KNOW YOU ARE SPEAKING AT THE RIGHT LEVEL?

Give a test speech in private to someone, or even a few people, who are at the same level as your future audience. Ask for their honest feedback. If they are all confused in the same places with the same things, you'll need to rework it until everyone can easily understand.

Tip: Record your presentation, give it a few days, and then listen to it. You'll hear specific areas where you may have stumbled a bit, or where the audience may have gotten confused.

On a whim, I attended a lecture on Darwin's theory of evolution by a Ph. D. in biology. I'm not a science major but I was interested in what the lecturer, a friend of mine, had to say. I expected a dry, factual presentation.

I couldn't have been more wrong. He had included funny pictures, facts, and tips while working in the scientific details. The information was fun, sassy, and easy to digest.

It left me thinking of evolution as a living, breathing, and very entertaining subject – not at all what I expected (by the way, he handed out Darwin cake at the end of his lecture too!).

My friend simply has a love of biology and wanted others to share it. He was an expert at connecting with the audience at our level while sharing his passion and expert knowledge of evolution.

Communication Tip #6 – Capture the heart and soul of your message and develop a human connection with your audience

If an audience has come out to see you, they want to like you, and they want you to like them. It's that simple – human beings want to be liked and accepted.

But an overload of dry data, facts, and statistics can easily make a person feel overwhelmed and can push people away because there's no emotional connection.

In the end, if you don't connect your heart and soul to your message, you'll fast-track your audience into unconsciousness and send your speaking career into the black hole.

If showing your love or passion for your subject makes you feel vulnerable, you're not alone, but that's also the key to what people connect to – the human element. *It can't be stressed enough how important it is to show your emotional intelligence.*

Finding the heart of your subject is as simple as asking yourself what you love about your topic. Why is it important enough for you to stand up in front of a room full of people? What got you excited about it in the first place? What makes you happy about sharing it with people?

How can the information you'll be presenting benefit your audience and make a positive impact in their lives?

So, find the heart and soul of your topic and let the audience like you.

Communication Tip #7 – Give your audience a call to action to help them change their lives for the better

Your audience members have come out to hear you speak because they want you to help them change their lives for the better. So help them do that!

If you haven't bothered to give them that significant question or challenge, you've failed your audience and are missing your mark as a speaker. Use the information you gave them during your talk to move them forward on a path of new and exciting thinking or behaviour.

A call to action supports the "close" in a sales pitch; it's the final and most necessary step in the presentation that tells your audience the next step they should be taking.

I recently hired a 17 year old country/western singer whose topic was to live your passion. She wove her words and music together to create a magical presentation. At her conclusion she ended with a question; "what's your passion, and what are you doing about it?" The message was one we'd heard many times before, but coming from the heart of this young singing sensation really brought it home. The audience was talking about it for weeks afterwards and posted their comments on Facebook.

Looking back on her second attempt at the same presentation, Leigh Miller couldn't help but feel proud of how far she had come. She had received some feedback from her colleagues and had immediately gotten to work on improving her presentation. This time, Leigh came in with a well-organized, simpler version of the same data and information.

Rather than trying to be all things to all people, she zeroed in on her specific niche, and had chosen to use a facilitated, interactive style rather than a lecture style. She had also worked in some simple choreography, and added some human stories to illustrate her points.

While she was presenting, she had felt herself relax and almost enjoy the experience. But even better, she noticed her audience was engaged in what she had to say – they had really listened and understood her.

At the end of her presentation, smiling people came up to thank her and to tell her how much they enjoyed her talk – and how much of a difference the information would make in their lives.

Even if your talk is informative – you can still come up with a call to action during your conclusion. Here are a few techniques for accomplishing that:

- *Give a handout with links to websites and blogs where they can leave comments or share information on how your topic helped them*

- *Provide a hashtag where they can tweet comments*

- *Ask a question that will stimulate the audience and further pique their interest*

- *Present a specific challenge or task for your audience to complete*

- *Suggest they elicit the help of a "buddy" to check in with and to enlist motivation and encouragement through email or phone support*

Doing these will connect your information with the audience, and keep you and your topic in their mind's eye long after they've left your seminar.

HOW TO WRITE A BRANDING STATEMENT:

What five words best describe what I do?

Example: *Inspire, create, motivate, transform, strategize*

Who is my target audience?

Example: *Job seekers who are stuck in a rut*

What makes me different from others providing a similar service?

Example: *I transform stuck career plans into vibrant opportunities*

What benefits do I provide?

Example: *I motivate, inspire, and provide strategies for career transformation*

What problem do I solve?

Example: *I turn stuck job seekers into motivated, professionals who are in charge of their career opportunities*

Bonus Point
Develop a Branding Statement

You might not like to think of yourself as a product like a Pop-Tart or an iPod, but developing a branding statement is as important in the speaking world as it is to Kellogg or Apple.

Look at it from the point of view of the consumer. If you were in charge of hiring a speaker for a seminar on career development, which of these speakers would you hire?

Speaker A: Author, Professional Speaker, Entrepreneur

Speaker B: I speak on marketing, sales and thinking big. Irreverent, unpredictable, knowledgeable, and funny, I am an empathetic speaker who likes to leave his audience a little smarter and thinking more like a skyscraper and less like a trailer.

Obviously, speaker B is the more desirable presenter. Consumers need to know exactly what you have to offer, and that's where branding comes in. It's also a chance for you to let your personality shine through.

Creating a branding statement is a natural part of knowing yourself. Take what you know about yourself and put it into one or two sentences – sometimes referred to as an "elevator pitch"– that explain who you are and what benefits you bring to your audience.

Before and after branding statements

A) "Don Brandless is an expert in career management and loves to talk about it."

B) "I inspire people to transform 'stuck' career management plans into vibrant opportunity creating strategies." – Career Coach Extraordinaire

After you've done your homework, it's a good idea to ask people who've worked with you to provide feedback. Ask them how they would describe you and see how their points of view might be used in your statement.

Also remember that a branding statement is often a work-in-progress, so revisit it regularly.

7 Ways Professional Speakers Avoid Looking Amateurish and Awkward on Stage

Although Leigh Miller knew she was doing better than her first and second attempts, she felt uncomfortable that parts of her presentation were still a little clunky.

At times her nerves got the better of her, and she wasn't sure how near or far away to stand from the microphone.

Then there was the PowerPoint projector that kept disconnecting from the computer and she wasn't sure what to do with her hands.

Stage Tip #1 – Work staging into your speech to avoid the "talking head" syndrome

Actors, singers, and dancers do it. So do savvy politicians and public figures of all kinds. They hire someone to work movements or "stagings" into their performances.

During these sessions, directors or acting coaches show them how to use the stage, their body, and facial expressions during their performances to make certain their physical message is the same as their verbal message.

Avoid walking/moving and talking at the same time – *walk first, talk later!*

If you are standing behind a podium – you can still use the above stagings, however, rather than walking, shift your body or eyes to centre, right, left, and back to centre, thereby mimicking the same movements described above.

So what does staging your performance do for you?

Using the stage to your advantage accomplishes several good things:

It creates the impression you are a seasoned professional completely comfortable using the entire stage and talking to each section of the audience.

Not everyone has access to an acting coach, but here are some simple techniques on how you can use the stage to map out your performance during your talk:

- Start centre stage with your introduction.

- Find a point to focus on (the top of someone's head is a good focal point – I never recommend looking right at a face during a talk. What if the person you are targeting has terrible indigestion and you interpret their sour expression as evidence they hate your talk?!).

- For the Body – take 2 steps to the right, stop, look in that direction – then deliver first part of the body of your talk.

OVERHEAD VIEW

- Take 2 steps to the left, stop, look in that direction – then deliver the 2nd point for the body of your talk.

- Stay where you are – look back to the right – deliver the 3rd section of the body of your talk.

GESTURES COME IN ALL SIZES:

Small – use when speaking to a smaller group or when speaking at a serious event. Small gestures are good if your audience is close to you and you are speaking on a smaller stage or speaking area.

Medium – use when speaking to a larger group or on a larger stage, and the audience is farther away from you.

Large – if you are speaking on a large stage to a big audience, gestures can be more exaggerated in order for the audience to see them.

• Walk back to centre stage, stop, look centre – deliver the conclusion of your talk.

• If your talk would benefit from it – you can also walk forwards, backwards, or shift up and down.

Stage Tip #2 – Use body language and props to enhance your message

Let's start with the basics.

Think of a gesture as using your body to add a picture to your words – much like putting an image into a PowerPoint presentation. Choreograph your gestures with the exact words you will be using so that they are meaningful. Then practice them many times.

The more often you practice, the more natural they will look and feel.

The general rule of thumb for gestures is the same for the use of props – only use them when you are making a point, or where your words/message would benefit from a picture or prop. The rest of the time, put them away.

Important: Recurring meaningless gestures (like the windshield wiper hands or hands jingling keys or change in a pocket) are annoying for the audience. So is holding a prop you are not using.

Doing these often will make the audience eventually tune you out!

Rehearsed movement is a great trigger for memory – your mind will associate the words you say with the physical movement you're making.

Movement creates an interesting visual for your audience.

Deliberate movement also shows your audience transitions between your points.

Using the stage also works as a memory tool for your audience members – they will associate the sections of your talk with the stagings you associated with the message. Also, it is more interesting for them to watch a speaker who has some movement rather than a speaker who stands, talks, and looks only in one place.

Also – don't forget your face!

People naturally look at faces to gain insight into the meaning of their messages. Therefore, your face needs to reflect the emotions of your message too.

Much can be written about mannerisms and gestures, and a good coach can help immensely in making sure your gestures and mannerisms support your message. But if you don't have access to a coach, a video will serve as an honest critic.

Record yourself and play it back, paying particular attention to your facial expressions, gestures, and mannerisms. Remember, a video can't lie or hurt your feelings. It's information for you to take in and use to your advantage.

Take note of where you could add gestures to support or emphasize your message. If you have recurring mannerisms (we all have some!) that would be best left out altogether, make a conscious effort to practice without them.

Play with adding gestures in places where your point could use emphasis. Play with smiling in certain spots or looking more serious, if needed. Attempt to put your whole body into your presentation.

When you have practiced a few times, record yourself again to watch how much you've improved!

Stage Tip #3 – Pay attention to your voice, tone, and inflections

Don't worry – I'm not going to get into the "breathing from the diaphragm" stuff here.

But you do need to sound like you – preferably a relaxed and genuine you. You won't be able to do that if you are feeling self-conscious about doing some goofy, vaguely worded exercise on top of and in addition to your speech.

Your voice is your signature. When you are happy, sad, or excited – people can hear it, and that's what you need to tap into. When you are involved in an animated conversation you communicate those feelings naturally.

You don't have to worry about projecting because you will have a microphone, so it's just a matter of taking yourself to a comfortable, conversational place where you can kick into auto pilot in public.

To break it down into a few simple mechanics (in case you go sideways), here are some simple things to do to help keep yourself on track:

- Concentrate on what you're saying – how does it make you feel? This is likely how it will make your audience feel as well.
- Imagine a close friend sitting in the front row and you are telling him/her your story. Does that make you feel more comfortable?
- **Adjust your volume** – You don't have to yell (unless it's part of your speech) but you can certainly keep your talk varied by emphasizing some words more than others with your volume level.
- **Play with the pace** – Typically, we speak faster when we're excited or happy and more slowly when we're serious. You can work that to your advantage in your performance.
- **Change your pitch** – Go higher to show excitement and lower to convey a more thoughtful topic.
- **Take pauses** – A pause in music has as much impact as sounded notes, and the same principle holds true in your speech. You don't need to fill the space with constant sound. Take pauses to emphasize a point, or allow the audience to take in your message and momentarily reflect on it before moving on to the next point.

After all that – if you really believe in your topic and are well prepared – you will do these things naturally. Remember – practice makes permanent.

HOW DO YOU GO ABOUT BEING YOURSELF ON STAGE?

Choose a topic you love and believe in – Speaking from the heart is what separates the A-level speakers from everyone else. If you don't love and believe in what you're talking about, your audience will see through you in a heartbeat.

Word it simply and honestly – If people want literary language they can read a James Joyce novel. When speaking to an audience simply talk in a conversational manner, as though you were speaking with a good friend.

Let your passion show – Showing passion embodies the words you choose, how you choose to deliver them, your body language, and stagings. All of it together exhibits the passion you hold in your heart for your subject matter. Let it shine through!

Be conversational – Similar to above, people just want to speak – and be spoken to – in a conversational manner. Keep industry-specific jargon to a minimum.

Add your own stories to support your message – Personal stories are powerful proof elements. If you have a personal story to support or validate your message, by all means incorporate it into your talk.

Stage Tip #4 – Let your unique personality shine through

Oscar Wilde once said: "Be yourself; everyone else is already taken."

What someone else does only works for them, not for you, and unless you can imitate that other person better than they can themselves – chances are your impression of them will fall flat.

Can you imagine David Letterman acting like Oprah or Ellen acting like Geraldo? It's a ridiculous thought, isn't it?

Yet, each of these very successful people found what they liked to do, how they liked to do it, enhanced it, and guess what? … it works for them and the people who love and support them.

Have you noticed how difficult it is to turn down a simple, honest request from a child? Just think of the last time you were able to say no to Girl Guide cookies or how you walked miles out of your way so you wouldn't cave when the kid in the grocery store asked you to buy hockey tickets.

A genuine, authentic "you" is what people will listen and respond to!

I used to teach communication classes with students at a technical college. Most had no experience with "public speaking" and were absolutely terrified.

To make it fun, I let them do their solo presentations on a topic of their choice with one activity that reinforced the topic and taught the audience something.

Car maintenance, cooking demonstrations, favorite children's books, gardening, safe sex, and Buddhism – nothing was off limits. When they spoke about their passions, (and were well prepared!) I heard amazing presentations from complete amateurs.

I was consistently blown away by how interesting, funny, and genuinely heartfelt they were. I still remember many of those presentations 15 years later.

Just being themselves and sharing their personal messages left a deep impact on me, further proving that these types of personal talks are the most powerful and moving talks you can present to an audience.

Stage Tip #5 – Embrace fear and focus your nervous energy

If you're human, and doing something new, you're going to be nervous. That's perfectly normal and you should expect it. If you plan to have nerves and have a couple of tricks up your sleeve, you'll be fine. If you don't plan for nerves, you can easily get derailed.

Give yourself plenty of time to get to your speaker engagement so that you arrive calm, and have time to check out the stage area and walk around. If possible, go in advance and do your own dress rehearsal.

When you are on stage – pause and smile at the audience (you'll notice they'll smile back). It's a good way to welcome them into your topic.

Before you talk – stop and think about what you will say in your introduction and conclusion. Then start your introduction.

If you get derailed – stop and collect yourself and keep going. Don't make a big deal about it and the audience won't either. In fact, they'll probably like you more because you've shown a human side they can relate to.

Bend your knees slightly and shift your weight to the front of your feet (while still keeping your entire foot on the ground). This will help to find your center, keep you grounded, and will relax you.

Remind yourself – the audience wants to like you and they want you to like them too!

When you've finished and are at home or a place where you can revisit – do a post mortem. What worked? What could work better? Write down your notes and work in what you learned, you'll discover you get better every time!

Once you know your talk, take advantage of some of the tips and tricks seasoned pro's use:

Memorize your introduction and conclusion – The start and end of your talk will be remembered more than anything else you say. Make sure they are memorized and rehearsed.

Focus on the message you want the audience to have and use – Remember, you are there to give them something useful... it's more about them, than it is about you!

Visualize – This is mandatory training for Olympic athletes and it really helps! Go through your entire talk in your head many times. Imagine yourself walking through your talk with stagings, smiling, feeling the emotions of your topic. Include the audience... see them in front of you smiling, enjoying your talk. Feel the feelings you would like to have during your talk – appreciation, enjoyment, acceptance... Imagine the audience's reaction at the end of your talk – clapping and cheering, on their feet wanting more. You can even imagine their comments when you're done. The more you do this, the more comfortable you will feel when you are on stage.

Stage Tip #6 – Include disaster planning time ahead of the speech date

There is always something that can or will go wrong the day of your performance – give yourself an hour or two of free time ahead of your performance to make time for minor disasters. Such as:

- Non-functioning microphone
- Wrong microphone
- Internet not working
- PowerPoint won't connect with your computer
- You're missing that critical extension cord to hook power to your computer
- Not enough tables
- The room has the wrong configuration
- The air conditioning unit is directly above the speaker's podium and you have to find someone in facilities to shut it off
- The room is freezing cold
- The room is too hot
- There are no stairs to the stage, and you don't want to pole vault up in high heels and a dress
- Something or someone critical didn't arrive and you need time to track it or them down

If something goes wrong and you've allowed for extra time, you'll be in good shape. If nothing goes wrong, even better! Either way, allowing for extra time to coat your nerves is a kindness you will want to give yourself.

Stage Tip #7 – Emulate and learn from professional speakers

If you want to watch some current speakers who blow your socks off, have a look at some of the Ted Talks on YouTube. These speakers move, inspire, motivate, and frequently bring their audiences to tears and to their feet in just 10-18 minutes.

Great speakers in history are another excellent way to learn – Martin Luther King, Winston Churchill, JFK, Abraham Lincoln, and numerous others had the ability to leave lasting impressions, even beyond their lives.

Churchill had a speech impediment and did not have a great speaking voice, yet his speaking style was emotional, authentic, and believable.

Think of some speakers you've heard who have left a lasting impression on you. Can you figure out what they do that works so well? You will start to notice their strengths when you analyze them.

Watch and analyze – some of what you learn from them will rub off on you. At the very least you'll come up with few new ideas of your own.

Watching videos of well performed speeches will help you in your learning process – and best of all, on the internet, it's free!

Another first-rate way to improve is to seek help from the experts – when you see someone like Oprah giving a talk to an audience of 10,000 – do you think for a moment she hasn't received coaching from the best of the best?! You bet she has.

Although people love her for all the great things she's done, they love her even more when she gives her audience an experience of a lifetime.

The two experts; great speakers, and a great coach can help you and your message create a meaningful experience that will make a lasting impact on your audience.

> *Leigh Miller felt like she was walking on air. She had invested in a few coaching sessions, and with additional practice with her equipment, her presentation was improving in leaps and bounds.*
>
> *Not only did she feel more comfortable, she knew what to do to get back on track if her nerves were jangling.*
>
> *She reviewed her checklist, she had arrived early, set everything up in advance, and walked through her performance with the gestures and stagings her coach had helped her with.*
>
> *After a number of practices and watching her own videos she felt confident in knowing her physical message was supporting her verbal message.*
>
> *Additionally, she found three YouTube Videos of favorite speakers who had inspired her to keep digging to find her own personality and presentation style. Leigh was starting to feel – and act! – like a seasoned professional.*

7 Critical Mistakes Speakers Must Avoid on and off Stage that Can Cause Embarrassment and Kill Repeat Business

Leigh Miller was smiling on the outside as she received the polite applause. On the inside, though, Leigh was upset. She knew that her talk didn't go as well as it could have gone.

It was an "okay" talk. But, Leigh knew that she could have done more to connect with her audience. She knew that her talk wasn't as personalized or engaging as it might have been.

And when she made that mistake about the biggest industry in town – she was mortified. No, as she walked offstage, Leigh Miller was disappointed in herself. She'd wanted to uplift and inspire the audience.

She wanted to move them emotionally with a strong call to action. Instead, she made some critical mistakes, and she knew it.

Mistake #1 – Failing to research and learn about the company that hired you

If you fail to do your homework on the company that hired you, you'll look unprepared, unprofessional, and likely ruin your chances of making a good first impression.

Imagine for a moment that you work in HR for a medium sized company. Your job is to arrange for speakers to come and give talks and workshops to the employees.

You hear of a speaker through the grapevine that is reputed to be "pretty good." So you hire this person to come and give a talk to your company. The day of the talk arrives, and the speaker shows up, but seems a bit confused.

He keeps calling you by the wrong name. He doesn't seem to know what your company actually does. As he steps out in front of the audience, your stomach sinks.

He clearly didn't read the information packet you sent him. This is not going to go well, and you're going to have to answer to your boss for hiring this speaker in the first place.

Don't be this guy! Don't put the person who hired you in the position of having to defend his or her choice.

One of the most basic mistakes a speaker can make is not doing research on the company that hired him or her. And what's worse is that this mistake is so easy to prevent!

It doesn't take that much time or effort to do a little bit of homework on your client. Doing so will allow you to talk knowledgeably both during your talk and when you're speaking with individuals before and after the event.

You'll be able to ask some insightful questions, build rapport, and learn more about your audience even before you step foot in front of them.

Your task therefore, is to find out about the company that hired you. What do they do? Who are the key players in the company?

Here are six questions for you to research and answer before you ever show up for your speaking gig:

1. *What is the vision and mission of their organization?*
2. *How long has the organization been in business?*
3. *What information can you access online? (Do they have a YouTube Channel, website, Facebook or LinkedIn page?)*
4. *What was their most successful speaker event and why?*
5. *What differentiates the company from their competitors?*
6. *Why are they hiring you? Are you part of a larger event? Is there some special expertise you have that the company is interested in learning more about?*

In order to find this information, you'll need to do two things. First, go online and enter the company name into a search engine. Look at their website, any news stories, press releases, and the like.

If the CEO was arrested recently, for example, that's a pretty important piece of information to have. Spend some time online looking at what the company says about itself and what others are saying about it.

Second, have a phone interview with the person that hired you. Take 15 minutes or so and ask the questions that can't be found on your own – such as #4, #5, and #6 above.

Once you've invested a little bit of time doing your homework, you'll be able to avoid making any embarrassing gaffes that come from not knowing enough about the company you're speaking to.

Google is still a great way to search for companies or individuals. Also many companies have LinkedIn and Facebook profiles. For reviews, check out Yelp.com.

Mistake #2 – Forgetting to tailor your talk to the audience, which will make you feel awkward and your audience feel uncomfortable and irritated

Now that you know about the company, it's time to focus on the audience. Who will be in attendance? After all, a company is comprised of many different groups of people.

A talk you give to a group of finance people will have a different tone and language level than a talk you give to a group of sales people in the same company.

You want to make sure that you tailor your talk to your audience. No one wants to feel as if they are getting the same talk that you gave 27 other times to other departments. And, saying "Hello Montreal!" at the beginning isn't sufficient!

The audience assumes you know what town you're in (and if you don't, that's a whole other story!). Show them that you cared enough to discover some things about them, and some answers they're looking for from you.

This comes from building rapport and by talking about things that are meaningful to the audience.

Here are three tips to build rapport/connection with your audience:

1. Find a way to work in a compliment during your opening greeting. For example, if you're talking to an audience from the shampoo industry, let them know you've used their products for X number of years.

   Tell them how your mother used to wash your hair with their shampoo (if it's true, of course) and you want to thank them for giving you some of your fondest memories through the use of their products.

   Alternatively, you can compliment their facility (if you're speaking on-site), or find some other genuine compliment you can give.

2. In your opening greeting, work in some current information about the city or industry that shows you are "in the know" about the area or industry and can appreciate their successes or struggles.

3. If you are good with humour – in your opening greeting, make a tasteful joke about a current issue from the community, or industry, or about issues all of us face as human beings. If you're not sure about the joke though, leave it out.

   There's nothing worse than an opening joke that falls flat!

When you take the time to make your talk specific to the audience you're speaking to, they feel an emotional connection with you and stay more engaged with your talk.

I was once asked to bring in a sports personality who was known for giving motivational talks. The IT College had mature students who were paying a large chunk of money to transition into a second or third career, and were very motivated to graduate.

When the speaker arrived, as I was escorting him to the front of the stage, he asked what kind of college it was, and was surprised the audience was not high school students.

He proceeded to give his "stay in high school" speech to the audience. The students looked confused and annoyed, I was cringing, and the speaker was embarrassed.

Needless to say, his talk fell flat.

All he would have needed to do was to tweak his talk slightly to the college listeners to have had the opposite effect – an appreciative audience.

Mistake #3 – Not knowing any information about – or worse, forgetting! – the city or town where you are speaking

It's every speaker's nightmare. You're up in front of the audience, looking out at all of the expectant faces smiling at you.

You smile, take a breath, and say, "Thank you! It's so wonderful to be here with you all in…" Your mind goes blank. Where am I? Is this Cincinnati? Or Cleveland?

I know it's somewhere in Ohio. You frantically scan the room for something—anything—that will give you a clue about the city or town you're in.

Finally, through an open door in the back of the room you can see the hotel sign out the window. Canton! I'm in Canton, Ohio!

While anyone's mind can go blank, if you've done your homework about the town you're visiting, you're far less likely to forget where you are.

Besides helping you remember the name of the city or town you're in, doing some research will help further your rapport with the audience. Every city has its local issues, flavour, and culture.

Failure to learn these details will result in a vanished opportunity to build a bond with your audience.

The more you know about the city or town, the more you can work relevant information into your talk. "I read this morning in The Herald that Elton John is coming to perform next month at the Ralph Engelstad Arena. How on earth did you guys pull that off?"

Don't rely on your airport driver to tell you about the town. Do your research in advance. Here are three areas that are a "must" when researching the city/town:

1. Are you in a city or town? What is the population?
2. What is the major industry?
3. What are three top newsworthy issues the city/town is facing?

Many cities have a version of their local newspapers online. In addition, you can often stream local radio stations through your computer. Listen to the news, the job report, or local talk radio to get a feel for the key things that the city or town is dealing with.

Make sure you check the local news the day before or the day of your talk. If something really important happened in the town, say an election, a major crime, or some other big event, you'll want to mention it in your talk. For example, after the Newtown, CT school shootings in December, 2012, many speakers, celebrities, and authors mentioned the incident in their speeches. But make sure to avoid taking a political stand. This isn't the time to advocate a position – just show that you're up on current events.

There is one important thing to note, though – keep your comments neutral. Don't take sides on any hot topic or political issue, or else you risk alienating some of your audience. Instead, try to choose topics that relate to your theme.

In the Elton John example mentioned above, you could tie in the fact that a small town who could get Elton John to perform can accomplish anything.

Choose news items that are relevant to what you're talking about and are not emotional triggers for audience members.

Mistake #4 – Expecting your client to handle all marketing and sales for your presentation

Expecting your client to handle all the logistics for your talk will create more work for your client and make you appear thankless. This is one of the mistakes that even the seasoned pros tend to make. After all, the client is the one who hired you. They should market you to fill their seats, right? Wrong.

If you've ever watched an afternoon or late night talk show, you know that the guests usually come on the show so that they can promote their latest movie, book, or event. If it's good enough for celebrities, politicians, and performers, it should work for you.

What are some ways you can effectively market your talks? The easiest approach is to have a calendar on your website with all of your speaking gigs on it.

Then, in all of your communications with your database, social media, and other marketing and publicity efforts, mention the talk. Send out press releases to the media sharing how your talk fits in with the others in the speaker series.

If your client has gotten you booked on radio talk shows, local television shows, or interviews with local newspapers, don't forget to name them in your interview!

Here are two tips that can help you incorporate information about your talk, your client, and the event into an interview:

1. Mention how happy you are to have been invited by the XYZ speaker organization to support their vision of _____ by sharing your knowledge about _____ (your talk/topic).

2. At the end of the interview thank the speaker organization again for inviting you to share in their vision of _____and let the audience know where the event is and where they can buy tickets.

Doing so will make your client organization happy, will help fill seats during the event, and will get your name in the public eye – which translates to more business for you.

> "Many a small thing has been made large by the right kind of advertising."
>
> MARK TWAIN

Mistake #5 – Not having a polished and up-to-date promotional package that you can send off immediately upon request

Time is money, and not having an up-to-date promo package ready to go at a moment's notice will annoy your client and create a traffic jam with the event deadline. Additionally, it will make you look amateurish.

"That's wonderful, Ms. Speaker. We are really looking forward to your talk next month. Can you send me a promo package this afternoon so that I can forward it to our advertising department?"

This is a common question I get all the time. After all, your client wants to get started with marketing materials. If you don't have a ready-made promotional package, this question can strike fear into your heart.

Therefore, it's your job to have a polished and up-to-date promotional package so that you can respond within seconds.

Don't make the mistake of thinking it's the client's job to wade through pages of your website and Google your name in order to come up with your bio, any more than it would be for a future employer to write your CV before an interview.

Here are five critical "must have" promotional materials that every speaker needs to have on hand:

1. Professional head shot in jpeg or gif format, and with low, medium, and high resolutions. Do not use a photo of you taken somewhere else.

   A professionally captured head shot sends the message that you're a professional speaker.

2. Professionally written biography: 100 words, 300 words, 500 –1000 words. You might even have more than one bio for different talks/audiences.

3. Professionally written branding statement – what do you do better than anyone else, and how are you identified?

4. Overview/outline of your talk – one page maximum in jpeg format, and a one sentence description of your talk.

5. References/testimonials in jpeg format.

The cost for a basic headshot photo shoot can range from $85-$750, with the average cost being between $200-$250. The pricing is usually time-based (60-90 minutes). Make sure to check if the price includes retouches and/or wardrobe changes.

Mistake #6 – Not rehearsing your performance which makes you look amateurish and ruins any chance of getting rehired

It's 7:00 am on the morning of your talk to the biggest audience you've ever spoken to. As you drive up to the hotel, you're feeling nervous and excited.

You get to the valet, only to realize that you have no cash and they don't take credit cards. You have to park at the lot down the street. Because of this, you have to make three trips to carry all of your equipment and materials.

When you finally get to the room, you note that there are only seats for half the expected number of attendees. Evidently, someone didn't get the memo that the divider between the two rooms was to be opened.

You get this corrected, but the stage is now off to only one side and the other side of the audience will need to turn their heads to see you. It's too late to fix it, so you'll have to make do.

As the audience members begin assembling, you're feeling flustered. You want to go over the notes one more time. But, where are they? Oh no! They're in the car. Down the street! You don't have any notes!

You did practice your talk last night a couple of times and once or twice in the car and on the plane. You'll do fine. Right?

Let's hope so because one of the biggest mistakes a speaker can make is not practicing and walking through every aspect of the performance in anticipation of these types of problems. The day of the talk is not the time to make sure everything goes smoothly.

Here are some things to make sure you do before the day of the talk:

- Practice the timing of your talk so that you don't run long or short.
- Limit the variables at the event as much as possible.
- Test your equipment the day before, or the day of your presentation, if possible.
- Practice your enunciation. If there are difficult words, complicated names, or foreign terms, make sure you are saying them correctly.

Here are five checkpoints to cover during your rehearsals to guarantee a seamless performance:

1. Practice your talk hundreds of times (yes, that's right...HUNDREDS) on your own, with your CD's, video clips, etc. Also, time it so that you know its exact duration.
2. Practice your talk in front of a couple of "test" audiences who you can trust to give you an honest assessment.
3. Practice your talk in front of a professional coach who can offer you professional feedback on your strengths, as well as tips for areas to improve, and tips for enjoying your time on stage.
4. Have your professional coach help you identify your body language, recurring gestures/ mannerisms and/or speech habits. We all have them. Once you are aware of them, you can easily eliminate them to make your body and speech congruent with your message.
5. Arrive early to get familiar and comfortable with the room, where the audience will be sitting, and to rehearse with all equipment.

Mistake #7 – Not following-up, failing to say thank you, and not requesting feedback after the speaker event

Failure to follow up, say thanks, and request feedback at the conclusion of your speaking event will tag you as having poor social skills and disinterested in improving your speaking skills.

Have you ever gone to a wedding? Surely you have. And, like most of us, you went to the store, printed out the wedding registry, and walked up and down the aisles looking for just the perfect gift.

Then, you wrapped the gift nicely and brought it to the wedding, stacked on the big table with all the other silver and white wrapped gifts.

But have you ever done all this and not received a thank you note?

If you've ever had the realization, "Hey, they didn't even say thank you!" then you know how important a thank you note is. Failure to write a thank you note can leave a very bad impression.

The fact is, even though you were paid to speak for the audience, the client was giving you a gift. Your client could have chosen any of the other thousands of people who would love a chance to speak to them.

So, following up with a thank you note is in order. Give a verbal thank you at the end of your talk and follow up with a note.

Another important item to do is to give a feedback form to both the audience and the client organization. It's a great way to get testimonials (always ask permission first) and get some important information on areas where you can improve.

No matter how excellent your speaking skills are, there is always room for improvement.

Here are three ways that guarantee you will be asked back again and recommended to others:

1. Thank the speaker organization at the beginning of the event.
2. Thank the speaker organization at the end of the event.
3. Thank the speaker organization the day following your event, pay them a sincere compliment about your experience, and let them know that you would be more than pleased to speak with them again. Mention you would appreciate them passing your name along.

Bonus Point #1 – Use valuable promotional materials to ramp up sales and ratchet up the fun!

Don't miss out on your opportunity to bring your promotional materials to the speaker event!

Although the organization may not allow you to sell your materials, you can always give one or two of your books, CD's, special reports, or products away as door prizes.

Giving away items does several things. It adds perceived value to the event – people love getting things for free.

It also generates curiosity for your products and services. It establishes credibility. And, it's fun!

Giving away raffles and door prizes adds energy and enthusiasm to your event.

You can also help your speaker organization create hype for your upcoming event by suggesting social media contests (Facebook, Twitter). Create a contest where people can win tickets, a book or other item, or something else that will create a buzz.

Even if the speaker organization doesn't use your social media promotional idea, they will appreciate your efforts.

Here are three ways to promote yourself during your speaker event:

1. Give away door prizes of one or two products before, during or after the event.
2. Audience prizes – everyone in the audience receives a product.
3. Facebook contests, where your product(s) are given away to very lucky contestants.

A few years ago, I hired a speaker who started her talk with quizzing the audience on easy facts about the speaker series. The first people who called out the correct answers won her books.

Not only did she reinforce our organizations' mission and vision, something I very much appreciated as the event organizer, she created a fun hype at the beginning of her talk for the audience.

She had us all eating out of the palm of her hand even before she began her talk.

Needless to say, I still remember and recommend her to other speaker organizations.

Bonus Point #2 – Match your wardrobe to the audience to build credibility and avoid insulting them

There's an old saying that "you can tell a lot about a man by his clothes." This is especially true in the public speaking arena. People naturally tend to trust and like those who are perceived as being "similar" to themselves.

A great way for you to do this is to match the style of your attire to that of the audience. This doesn't mean you wear a college sweatshirt if you're speaking to university students, but you probably don't want to wear a three-piece suit, either.

Similarly, if you're speaking to a group of investment bankers, you'll want to avoid wearing jeans and a short sleeved shirt.

Also, do a quick mirror check right before going in front of the audience. Make sure your hair is combed, there is no food in your teeth, that your zipper is closed, and that you look the way you want to.

I knew someone who gave an entire talk with a piece of paper towel stuck to his forehead that he was unaware of. Talk about distracting!

Here are four ways to make sure your attire matches that of your audience:

1. Revisit the research you did in avoiding Mistake #1. What's the culture of the group you're speaking to?

2. Take everything out of your jacket and/or pants pockets prior to speaking. It's too easy to fiddle with things when you're talking and that's distracting to the audience.

3. Avoid wearing anything with writing on it or overly complicated images. Otherwise, your audience will be trying to figure out what that symbol is on your tie instead of listening to your message.

4. To avoid wardrobe malfunctions (e.g. a price tag under your arm, a shirt/dress that rides up from static cling, or heels that give you trouble walking), never wear a new outfit.

Appendix/Worksheets
Audience Research Form

What is the demographic of your audience?

• Is the majority of your audience made up of men or women?

_____
_____
_____

• What are their occupations? Are they from a specific industry or various industries?

_____
_____
_____

• What is the average age of your audience members?

_____
_____
_____

• Is your speaker event a work related event or is it for personal growth?

_____
_____
_____

• Is your audience dressed formally or casually?

_____
_____
_____

• Is the venue formal or casual?

_____
_____
_____

• How near or far away is your audience from where you will be presenting? Will you be standing close to them (in a conference room/dinner/luncheon/classroom venue) or up on a stage behind a podium?

_____
_____
_____

City/Town Research Form

- What is the name of the city or town where you will be speaking?

_____

_____

- What is the population?

_____

_____

_____

- What is the major industry of the city/town?

_____

_____

_____

- What local news events are most important from the day/week before your talk?

_____

_____

_____

- What are noteworthy items about the city/town you could find that would show you as being "in the know" about the area? For example, cultural events, fairs/tradeshows, anything specific to the city/town that can't be found elsewhere? Find three important facts.

_____

_____

_____

_____

_____

_____

Speaker Organization Research Form

1. What is the vision and mission of the organization?

_____

_____

2. How long has the organization been in business?

_____

3. What information can you access online to give you an overview and history? (Do they have a YouTube channel, website, Facebook, or LinkedIn page?)

_____

_____

4. What is the focus of their speaker events? Why are they running a speaker series, a conference or workshop?

_____

_____

_____

5. What was their most successful speaker event and why?

_____

_____

6. What differentiates the company/speaker organization from their competitors?

_____

7. Why are they hiring you? Does your talk fit into a speaker theme? Are you part of a larger event? Is there some special expertise you have that the company is interested in learning more about?

_____

_____

_____

8. How many speaker events per year do they host?

_____

9. Is this a luncheon or dinner event?

_____

10. Is there a networking component to this event? If there is, is there an expectation you participate or contribute to it? If so, how?

_____

_____

Presentation Outline

1. Introduction

• Grab the audience's attention and warm them to your topic
• Show your audience what's in it for them by using one of the techniques below:
  Telling a story
  Asking a question
  Using a quote
  Telling a joke/using humor
  Demonstrating something

_____

_____

_____

_____

2. The body – middle – main section of your talk:

  POINT #1 _____

  Sub point #1 _____

    Transition _____

  POINT #2 _____

  Sub point #2 _____

    Transition _____

  POINT #3 _____

  Sub point #3 _____

    Transition _____

3. The conclusion – summarize your point/theme + call to action

  POINT 1+2+3 = conclusion

_____

_____

_____

_____

_____

Call to Action
• Ask a question
• Present a challenge

Post-event feedback form

• What interested you? What did you find helpful during this topic/talk?

_____

_____

_____

_____

• How did you hear about this event/speaker? Example: e-vite, poster, Facebook, LinkedIn, radio ad, newspaper ad?

_____

_____

_____

_____

• What learning will you take with you into your personal life or to work?

_____

_____

_____

_____

• Are there any areas requiring improvement, if so please explain.

_____

_____

_____

_____

• Was attending this event beneficial, and if so, would you bring others with you to the next event and/or recommend the series?

_____

_____

_____

• Additional comments/suggestions?

_____

_____

_____

_____

Promotional Package

☑ **Professional head shot in jpeg or gif format**, and with low, and high resolutions. Low and medium formats are used for most web-based media; Facebook, websites, and LinkedIn profiles, whereas high resolution is used for anything printed such as posters, newspaper articles, flyers, etc.

☑ Ensure your photo presents you as a **professional**, in dress appropriate to your profession. For example, if you are a speaker who motivates businesses to realize greater profits, you will want to be seen in a business suit. However, if your talk is about fitness techniques for personal trainers, your picture should show you in workout wear.

☑ Professionally written **biography**;
   a. 100 words (a very brief overview of who you are, and what you offer. This could be used as a caption on an e-vite, Facebook promo, or even on a poster.
   b. 300 words (who you are, what you offer, and supporting details). This length of bio could be used on a webpage description, or sent to potential clients who are wanting to know more about the event.
   c. 500 –1000 words (a full professional biography/summary of your professional achievements). This type of bio can be utilized in conference materials, your own personal webpage, or for a feature article. You might even have more than one bio for different talks/audiences.

☑ Professionally written **branding statement** – what do you do better than anyone else, and how are you identified? In one – three sentences only.

☑ **Overview/outline** of your talk – a one sentence description of your talk at the top, followed by one page maximum in jpeg format with numbered topic areas and 1 – 3 bulleted points under each topic header.

☑ **References/testimonials** in jpeg format. Either scan or copy these on to one page or with quotation marks around the comments and the person's name underneath (to show credibility).

Sample Biographies

100 Word Bio: Jane Doe

Jane Doe is an award winning speaker, author, trainer, and executive coach. Her laser-focused, high calibre, energetic programs are highly practical, easy to implement, fun, and memorable.

In 2003, the Canadian Business Advisory Council named Ms. Doe, "Canadian Business Person of the Year" and her company Talent Drive International received a "Sphere of Excellence" Award from the Calgary Chamber of Commerce.

Jane is an accomplished author with three books to her credit including; Your 7 Best Employees... 47 Creative Ways to Ignite your Staff to Greater Heights, and Jump Start your Employee Success.

Jane Doe, janedoe@yahoo.com, (000) 000-9999

300 Word Bio: Jane Doe

Jane Doe is an award winning speaker, author, trainer, and executive coach. She has presented keynote speeches, workshops, and seminars in 17 countries on five continents. Her laser - focused, high calibre, energetic programs are highly practical, fun, and memorable.

Prior to becoming a full-time professional speaker, Doe was a successful entrepreneur. She built the first "GirlPwr" boutique with a $2000 investment and in 2003, the Canadian Business Advisory Council named Ms. Doe, "Canadian Business Person of the Year" and her company Talent Drive International received a "Sphere of Excellence" Award from the Calgary Chamber of Commerce.

In 2002, Jane founded Talent Drive International, a training and development company with headquarters in Calgary, Alberta. As President of Talent Drive International, she motivates and inspires her organization to greater success with her passion to create meaningful, value-based change to both the individuals and the organizations she serves.

Jane is an accomplished author with three books to her credit including; Your 7 Best Employees... 47 Creative Ways to Ignite your Staff to Greater Heights, and Jump Start your Employee Success... a handbook for the talent management business sector.

A strong advocate for volunteering, Jane serves as chair of the board of Executive Women Volunteers for Youth, a post she has held since 1998. As chair of the board of Executive Women Volunteers for Youth (EWVY), Jane strives to create mentorship and leadership opportunities matching young women with established women in businesses across the country. In collaboration with EWVY, Jane has helped raise over two million dollars for a variety of charitable Canadian organizations.

Since 2000, she has presented keynote speeches, workshops, and seminars to over 1700 audiences, most of them repeat engagements. This includes Fortune 500 companies and many International associations. Her coaching clients include CEO's, Presidents and Vice Presidents, executives, entertainers, and government officials.

Jane Doe, janedoe@yahoo.com, (000) 000-9999

500 Word Bio: Jane Doe

Jane Doe is an award winning speaker, author, trainer, and executive coach. She has presented keynote speeches, workshops, and seminars in 17 countries on five continents. Her laser-focused, high calibre, energetic programs are highly practical, fun, and memorable. Since 2000, she has presented keynote speeches, workshops, and seminars to over 1700 audiences, most of them repeat engagements. This includes Fortune 500 companies and many private companies.

Prior to becoming a full-time professional speaker, Doe was a successful entrepreneur. She built the first "GirlPwr" boutique with a $2000 investment and in 2003, the Canadian Business Advisory Council named Ms. Doe, "Canadian Business Person of the Year" and her company Talent Drive International received a "Sphere of Excellence" Award from the Calgary Chamber of Commerce. Since 2003, Jane has established 500 GirlPwr scholarships for women in post-secondary education, and has donated over $500,000 to GilPwr in Action, a high school education program which provides leadership opportunities to young women aged 13-18. Additionally, at GirlPwr, Jane established a women's leadership in action workplace group, designed to help women advance both personally and professionally.

In 2002, Jane founded Talent Drive International, a training and development company with headquarters in Calgary, Alberta. As President of Talent Drive International, she motivates and inspires her organization to greater success with her passion to create meaningful, value-based change to both the individuals and the organizations she serves. Since 2003, Jane has traveled extensively around the country, working as a trainer and consultant with audiences ranging from housewives and college students to CEOs. She has helped thousands of businesses rebuild their employee morale and create successful working cultures. Her clients include; CEO's, Presidents, Vice Presidents, executives, entertainers, and government officials.

Jane is an accomplished author with three books to her credit including; Your 7 Best Employees... 47 Creative Ways to Ignite your Staff to Greater Heights, and Jump Start your Employee Success... a handbook for the talent management business sector.

A strong advocate for volunteering, Jane serves as chair of the board of Executive Women Volunteers for Youth (EWVY), a post she has held since 1998. As chair of EWVY, Jane strives to create mentorship and leadership opportunities matching young women with established women in business. To date, EWVY has successfully matched over 500 mentors with mentees. Many mentees have realized career success through this collaboration, and have gone on to become mentors. 95% of mentors remain with EWVY five years or more.

From 2004 to 2011, Jane and Executive Women Volunteers raised over $2 million for multiple charitable organizations, including the Women and Memory Foundation, Children's Help Hospice, and the Just Read, library foundation.

In addition to her business and volunteer activities, Jane is an avid cycler and yoga enthusiast. John Small, Founder of the prestigious Speakers Association of Canada, of which Jane is a member, said "Her message is always impactful, brilliantly simple, and yet motivating and fun. The stories she shares support her message seamlessly. I can't wait to hear what she has to say next!"

Jane Doe, janedoe@yahoo.com, (000) 000-9999

Introduction

Jane Doe

Our guest speaker, Jane Doe, is President of Talent Drive International, a performance talent management company that offers training and consulting in decision making, leadership skills, change management and diversity in the workplace.

She is co-author of the books, Your 7 Best Employees... 47 Creative Ways to Ignite your Staff to Greater Heights, and Jump Start your Employee Success.

In 2003, the Canadian Business Advisory Council named Ms. Doe, "Canadian Business Person of the Year" and her company Talent Drive International received a "Sphere of Excellence" Award from the Calgary Chamber of Commerce.

To speak to us today on the topic of _____ please help me welcome today's guest speaker... Ms. Jane Doe

Sample Room Configurations

The room setup will depend on several factors;

- The size and shape of the room
- The size and type of the audience
- The type of presentation and delivery method you choose
- The type of interaction you want from your audience

There are basically six styles of audience configurations:

Auditorium style

This is best for large groups when doing a keynote presentation and when the audience is not required to participate or interact.

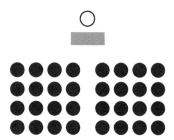

Classroom style

This is a good configuration for information situations where the audience members are required to participate and interact.

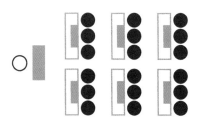

Conference style

This is a good configuration for small groups who will have a high degree of interaction with each other. Typically there is a meal being served.

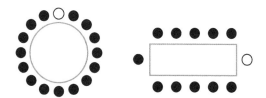

Horseshoe/u-shape style – rectangle

This is a good informal configuration when the facilitator and the participants are required to maintain a high degree of eye contact with each other.

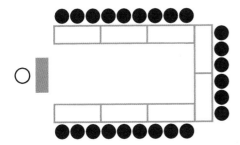

Horseshoe/u-shape, semi-circular

This is a good informal, interactive style that encourages a high degree of participation.

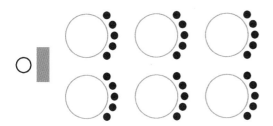

Herringbone style

This is a useful configuration when you require group discussions/participant interaction. It is a little more formal than a Horseshoe style.

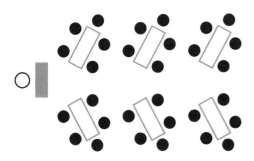

Presentation Planning Worksheet

Presentation topic: _____

Presenter/s: _____

Event coordinator: _____

Event co-ordinator contact information: _____

Presentation date: _____ Time: _____

Address/building: _____ Room number: _____

Building site contact person: _____

Phone/email: _____

Audience:

Number of audience members: _____

Preferred presentation style: _____

Room Set-Up:

❏ Auditorium   ❏ Conference   ❏ Horseshoe – rectangular   ❏ Classroom

❏ Horseshoe – semi-circle   ❏ Herringbone   ❏ Other: _____

30123843R00023

Made in the USA
Charleston, SC
02 June 2014